GROWING OLDER

Lesley Newson

Contents

A&C BLACK · LONDON

SCIENCE MYSTERIES

Everyone's destiny

What do you want to do with your life? You will have many choices to make as you grow older. But there is one thing you will have no choice about: you will grow older. Your body will get bigger and you will go through many changes. There is nothing you can really do to make yourself grow faster or more slowly. Your body seems to be programmed to live a life that is more or less the same as every other person's life: you will grow up, you will grow old and you will die.

Yet there are differences too. Some girls start having periods when they are still in primary school while others don't begin until they are well into secondary school. Some fourteen year-old boys still look and sound like boys; others have deep voices and the beginnings of beards.

Through all of human history, people have followed the same basic path through life.

As people grow older, the differences mount up. Some forty year-olds seem to look, feel and act just like someone in their twenties. Others are already complaining of aching joints and feeling tired all the time. Some people seem frail and forgetful by the time they're sixty. Others are still working and playing hard when they are in their eighties. Some people have long, happy and healthy lives; others die young.

For thousands of years, people have wondered how much of their life is programmed in advance and how much of it is under their control. Does each person have a life plan? Is it possible to read it? Can it be altered? Could it be completely rewritten so that no one ever has to grow old and die?

People have always looked to the wisest people in the community to help them work out answers to these questions about life. Religious teachers, philosophers, great writers and, more recently, scientists have all had ideas about why people seem to be destined to live life in a certain way. They have made suggestions about what humans may be able to do to change their destiny.

For people who are lucky enough to stay healthy, old age is a time of continuing achievement.

Medical advances such as immunisation have given us a bit more control over our destiny.

Today, we have more power than ever before to change our destiny. By investigating the causes of illness, scientists have helped to find ways of curing or preventing diseases that used to kill millions of people. Scientists have also learned a great deal about what happens to the human body as people grow older. They are beginning to understand how our bodies are programmed to follow a certain life plan and how it may be possible to alter the programme.

This book is about what has been learned so far about the programme we follow as we grow older and about the many mysteries that remain.

The wisdom of the past

The writings and stories created by our ancestors show how deeply they pondered the mysteries of life. One way they made sense of it all was to invent stories to explain the way life seemed to be.

Thousands of years ago, the people of Greece thought the world was ruled by many gods and goddesses. Three of the most powerful were the goddesses of destiny, known as the three Fates. They knew the past and the future and decided each person's life plan. It was laid down at birth and could not be changed.

The Fates

The Ancient Greeks believed that our lives and destiny are controlled by the three Fates: Clotho, Lachesis and Atropos, shown here in a Flemish 16th-century tapestry. When a person was born, the first Fate, Clotho spun the thread of life for that person. The second Fate, Lachesis, measured a certain length. The third Fate, Atropos cut the thread at the end of life.

So, for the ancient Greeks and some other cultures, it didn't seem worthwhile to try to change what life had in store. Other cultures taught that people do have some control of their destiny. They believed that working hard and being kind would bring a happier life and that carelessness, greed and gluttony would lead to injury and disease. People who suffered misfortune did sometimes seem to deserve it, but just as often, life seemed to be very unfair.

In many cultures people began to teach that fairness would come after death, when good would be rewarded and wicked people would be punished.

The Hindu religion teaches that when the body dies its soul passes into the body of a new baby.

Throughout history, human beings have tried to explain their existence and find a meaning for it. For many people, the human life plan only makes sense if it is part of a much bigger plan. They believe that once a person's body has lived out its programme of growing up, growing old and dying, the person's soul or self leaves the body and continues with the larger life plan. Christians, Jews and Muslims, for example, are taught that there is a God who cares about people and how they behave. For them, the larger life plan is God's plan and if people follow that plan they will be rewarded after they die by being allowed to live in happiness with God.

Hindus and Buddists believe that souls or parts of the human personality live many lives on Earth in many different bodies until they are ready to join the mysterious universal spirit.

About 500 years ago, some of our ancestors began exploring new ways of pondering the mysteries of life. Instead of just thinking about the sky, the Earth and living things, they began carefully to examine them. They conducted experiments. Slowly, over the centuries, people who became known as 'scientists' built up a better understanding of living things and the life plans they follow.

The simplest life forms

Although all living things grow, not all of them grow older. Most living things are made up of a single cell and can only be seen with a microscope. They follow life plans that are much simpler than ours, but scientists have learned a great deal about all life by studying these simple creatures.

Bacteria are single-celled creatures. Each cell absorbs food, grows and in time splits to become two bacteria that are identical or nearly identical to the original. If they have a rich supply of food, some bacteria are able to double their numbers in less than 20 minutes. Overnight, a few bacteria can become a population of billions. A cloth soaked in disinfectant can, of course, wipe out almost all of them in seconds. Even so, because they are simple and because there are so many of them, bacteria can be very hardy too. A population of bacteria can be left without food, frozen solid or completely dried out, and some will still survive. Bacteria have been found frozen in Arctic glaciers. They must have been there for thousands of years yet, once thawed out and given food, some of them were able to start growing.

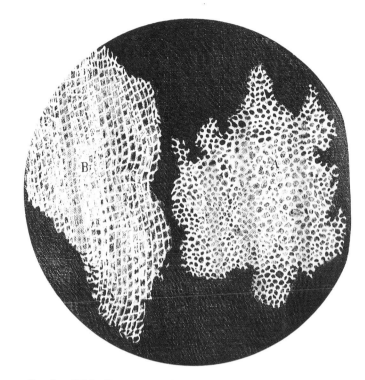

In the 17th Century, scientists caught their first glimpse of a new world of life. With magnifying lenses, they saw a vast range of creatures invisible to the naked eye. They also saw the minute yet complex structures that make up all living things. In 1665, a British scientist named Robert Hooke published Micrographia, *a book of drawings of things he had seen using a microscope. This drawing is of a thin slice of cork. Hooke saw that it was divided into tiny chambers which he called 'cells'.*

There are many single-celled creatures that are larger and more complicated than bacteria. The micro-organisms called yeast, which are used to make bread rise, are one example. Like bacteria, yeast can survive conditions that would kill an animal or plant. Dried yeast is sold in packets in shops. Just add warm water and it comes back to life. Most of the time yeast cells reproduce by simply splitting in two, but they can follow more complicated life plans too. Two can join together to make a double cell. These can go on splitting in two as double cells or they can join with another double cell and then separate into four single daughter cells, each slightly different from its four parents.

New yeast cells being 'born'. They simply form as 'buds' that separate from their parent cell.

Life's basic plan

There are many different kinds of living things on earth. Each kind follows its own life plan but in some very basic ways, the plans are the same. Everything that is alive:

- *Takes in energy and material from the environment.*

- *Makes more of itself by growing larger and by making more living things which are similar to itself.*

- *Keeps itself separate from the environment.*

- *Is a cell or group of cells. Cells contain the machinery that does this life work, machinery so tiny and so complex that it makes the micro-electronics in a portable computer seem clumsy and enormous.*

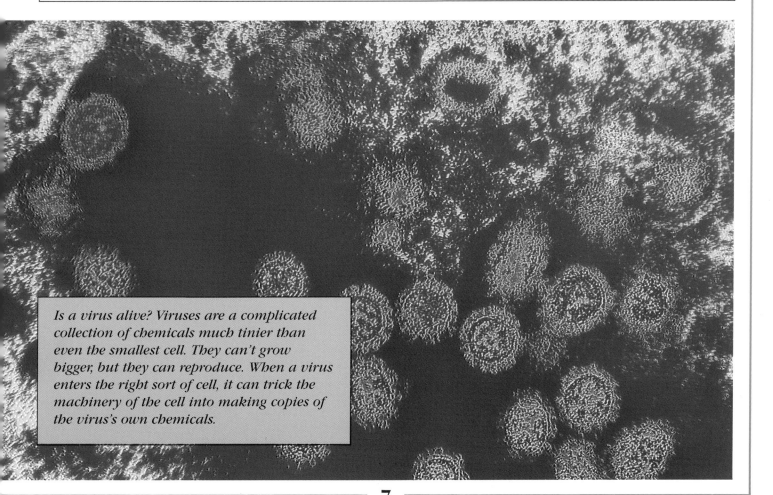

Is a virus alive? Viruses are a complicated collection of chemicals much tinier than even the smallest cell. They can't grow bigger, but they can reproduce. When a virus enters the right sort of cell, it can trick the machinery of the cell into making copies of the virus's own chemicals.

Creatures that are made up of many cells need a more complicated life plan than single-celled organisms. If you think of a single-celled organism as being like a craftsman in his workshop, a multi-celled creature is like a huge factory with many workers. There are different kinds of workers doing different jobs but they are all working together. Just like a factory, a creature with many cells has to be well organised.

Among the simplest multi-cell creatures are sponges. The billions of cells that make up a sponge are of only three basic types: structure cells, feeding cells and reproductive cells.

Sponges

A sponge is a simple multi-celled organism. It has only three types of cell.

The first type (1) makes the structure of the sponge, forming the tough fibres that hold the sponge cells together in a shape and anchor them to the sea floor. Sponges can be different sizes and shapes but they all have a tube or tubes which they use to collect their food.

The second type of sponge cell (2) lives in the walls inside the tubes. Its function is to collect food. Each food collector cell has a tail which it waves constantly. This movement makes water flow through the sponge so that the cells can grab single-celled creatures and other tiny bits of food which are floating in the water. The food is broken up and released to all the cells of the sponge.

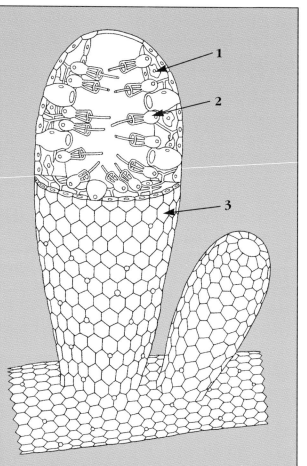

The job of the third kind of cell (3) is to make new cells so the sponge can grow. While food is plentiful, these cells grow and split in two. Then the new cells change into either structure-making cells or food collectors. Scientists call this changing 'differentiating'.

The yellow chimney sponge is only one of over 5000 different kinds of sponge which live in the world's oceans.

Plants are made up of many more different types of cells than sponges, but the life plan they follow is similar in some ways. Plant cells organise themselves into basic shapes like a stem, a branch, a leaf or a flower and as the plant grows, that shape is repeated again and again. By pruning and clipping, a skilful gardener can control the way a plant grows to make it bushier or to grow more flowers.

People who enjoy growing house plants know that you don't always need to grow a new plant from a seed. A leaf or branch cut from many kinds of plant will soon grow roots if it's placed in water or moist soil. That's because, like sponges, plants contain cells that can differentiate into any of the types of cells that make up the whole plant. Biologists have found they can grow these cells in the laboratory in special mixtures of nutrients. They grow into shapeless lumps of millions of cells, but if they are treated with special plant chemicals, they begin to form themselves into tiny new plants.

These plants have grown from a lump of plant cells which were placed in a jelly containing nutrients and special chemicals to make the cells differentiate.

Making babies

The cells that work together to make an animal follow a more complex life plan than those of plant cells. As a plant grows, its cells differentiate and are programmed to organise themselves into leaves, flowers and stems. But the precise way that the plant will grow is not programmed in advance. A pine tree can be bent or straight, bushy or spindly. It can be made to grow as a miniature bonsai tree.

Animals, however, are all destined to grow in a certain way. The cells of animals are programmed to differentiate and organise themselves to make a whole creature of a certain size and shape. The eggs laid by a fly are destined to grow into something shaped exactly like a fly. When a mare and stallion mate, their baby will be horse-shaped.

Some of the greatest minds in history have tried to puzzle out how new animals come about, how babies are made. They knew it was something to do with having sex. That part of the story was worked out in prehistoric times.

They are both horse-shaped but Shire horses are destined to grow much larger than Shetland ponies.

But they didn't know why sex caused a baby to start to grow inside a woman. Understanding this became possible in 1839 when two German scientists named Matthias Schleiden and Theodor Schwann worked out that humans, like other large animals, are made up of billions of cells.

Countdown to a baby

The cells of a growing animal follow a life plan that makes them change as time passes so the animal grows up in exactly the right way. Your cells, like the cells of all animals, are following a schedule. Somehow, your cells know what they are supposed to be doing at each stage of your life.

Time 0:
The schedule begins at a moment called 'conception' or 'fertilisation' when an egg made by your mother joins with a sperm made by your father to make a single ball-shaped cell about 0.15mm in diameter.

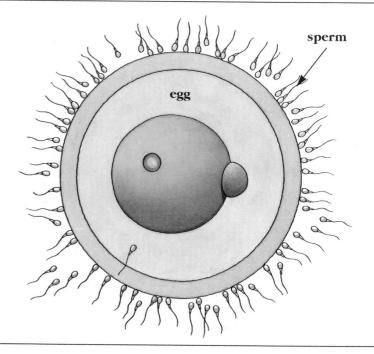

As well as their body cells, animals make sex cells and these are what make new babies possible. When two of these cells unite, a new cell is formed and from this single cell, a new animal grows. The way that new baby animals grow and develop is surprisingly similar in many different species. In humans and many other animals, the sex cell of the female is larger and is called an egg. The male sex cells, called sperm, are tiny; they are produced in great numbers and they can swim.

When an egg and sperm unite, the new cell is called a 'fertilised' egg. A fertilised egg that is developing into an animal is called an 'embryo' and scientists who study this development are called 'embryologists'. A human embryo, like the embryos of other mammals, can only develop inside its mother so it's only possible to catch glimpses of living human embryos but embryologists have been able to learn about how new humans develop by looking at human embryos that have died and by studying the living embryos of animals like chickens, toads, flies and sea urchins which naturally develop outside their mother's body. They have found that there are many similarities in the development of all animal embryos.

As this fertilised frog egg begins its second division, it is following a plan similar to that of human eggs and the eggs of all animals.

24 hours:
Your single cell splits in two. Each is about half the size of the fertilised egg but they seem to be the same in every other way. If these two cells had broken apart, each one would have grown into a baby. The babies would look the same and would be called identical twins. Every few hours after this, the cells split in two again.

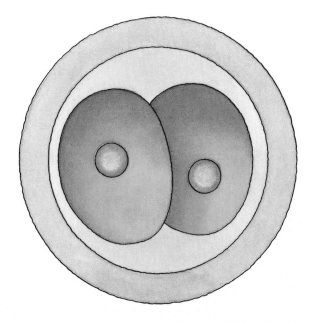

Biologists have invented many ways of closely observing what is going on when a new animal develops and, the more they see, the more amazingly complex it appears. The first fertilised egg cell divides to make more cells. They grow and divide some more. But how does this mass of cells become a baby? The answer is that the cells all seem to 'know' what to do. They differentiate to do different jobs and move around and organise themselves into a baby.

For a scientist, watching cells in a developing embryo is a bit like seeing a complicated ballet. Each cell is a dancer and there are millions of them. They move at exactly the right time to meet up with cells from another part of the embryo. Once they meet they must know the exact steps to take together to make the organs and tissues of the future baby's body. Cells must also die on cue when the part they play is finished.

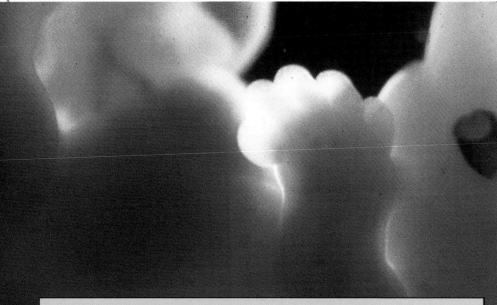

When a human embryo is eight weeks old it is time for the fingers on the embryo's hand to separate. As if on cue, all the cells which have been holding the fingers together die, allowing the hand to be formed.

Who is the choreographer of this microscopic ballet? How do the cells know what to do? Part of the answer lies in the 'genetic information' of which every cell has a copy. These are instructions which the cells follow to make the complicated substances that make up the body. A baby inherits these instructions from its parents, half from each of them. They come together when the egg and sperm join to make the first cell of the baby's body. In this new cell the instructions are combined in a new way, but they are instructions which have been copied and passed down millions of generations.

5 days:
You are a ball of several hundred cells and are ready to burrow into the soft lining that has grown on the inside wall of your mother's womb. Your cells have already begun to differentiate. Those on the outside of the ball form a connection with your mother's blood vessels as a means of obtaining food so that you can begin to grow larger. The cells on the inside are destined to become you.

2 weeks:
The cells which will become you have formed themselves into a disk and suddenly they begin to move. Those on the surface of the disk start to dive down a slit in the centre. They spread out inside to form three layers, each made up of a different kind of cell. These are each destined to become a different part of your body.

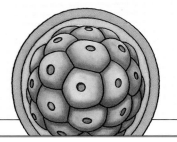

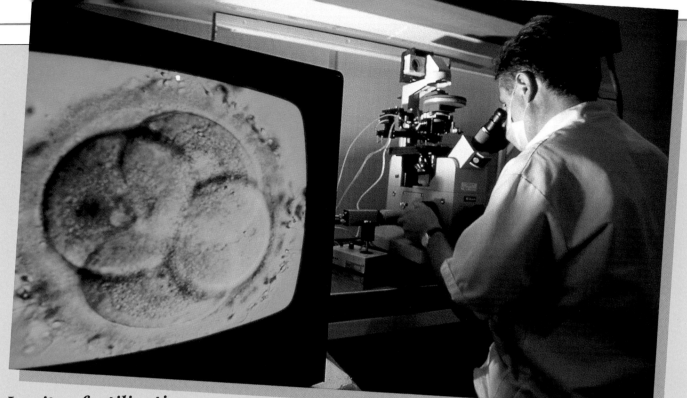

In vitro fertilisation

The living human embryo shown on this television screen is about a day old. For most human babies, fertilisation happens inside the mother's body, but some women have blockages in tubes just above the womb called 'fallopian tubes', which prevent the father's sperm from reaching the mother's egg. To help these couples to have children, doctors and scientists have developed a way of keeping human eggs, sperm and embryos alive outside the body for a short time. This embryo was made by 'in vitro fertilisation' or IVF, which means it was fertilised in a plastic dish. It has now divided twice to become four cells and will shortly be placed in its mother's womb in the hope that it will grow into a baby. IVF doesn't always work but it has helped thousands of childless couples have babies.

3 weeks:

Your cells start to organise themselves into the beginnings of your brain and spine. Your heart has begun to beat and blood is starting to move around your body.

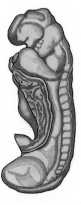

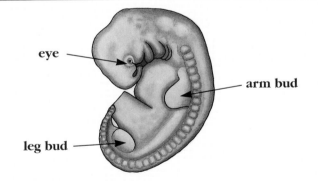

eye

arm bud

leg bud

5 weeks:

You still don't look much like a baby, but the most important and complicated parts of making you are now over. Your cells have differentiated into most of the 200 or so different types of cell that will make your body. You are far from ready to be born though.

The fact that the cells carry genetic instructions doesn't explain how they manage to organise themselves into a baby, though. How do they know which instructions to follow and when? Part of the answer may lie in the way cells communicate with each other. Scientists have found that cells are continually releasing chemicals which act as signals to their neighbouring cells and sometimes to cells in distant parts of the body. There are also chemicals attached to the outside of cells that act as labels. As certain cells touch, they seem to be able to 'read' each other.

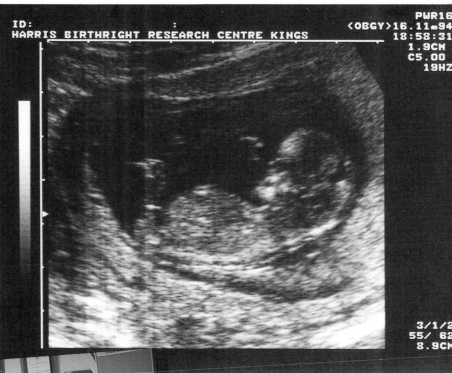

ID: :   PWR16
HARRIS BIRTHRIGHT RESEARCH CENTRE KINGS   <OBGY>16.11m94
                                                        18:58:31
                                                          1.9CM
                                                          C5.00
                                                           19HZ

3/1/2
55/ 62
8.9CM

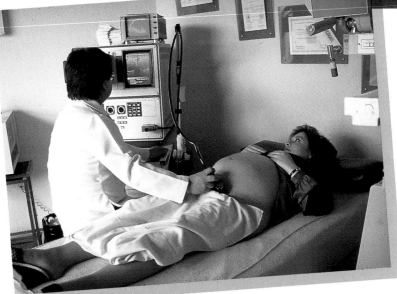

This image of a 12-week old baby, called a fetus, was made by scanning its mother's womb with a beam of ultrasound. Ultrasound doesn't harm the fetus and scans are useful for letting parents and doctors know how the baby is developing and gives early warning if the baby needs extra medical help.

18 weeks:
The movements you are making are now big enough for your mother to feel.

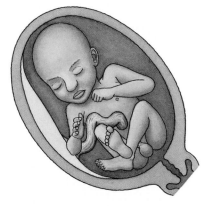

10 weeks:
It is now possible to tell by looking at you if you are a girl or a boy. You were destined to be the sex you are from the moment the egg and sperm joined to make your first cell. Boys develop a penis and testes. Girls develop a vulva, vagina, womb and ovaries. These have been developing inside you for several weeks but now your vulva or your penis is visible.

When you think how complicated making babies is, it seems incredible that most babies are delivered on time and in perfect condition. Babies make themselves and, before her baby is born, all the mother has to do is provide it with a good environment to grow in. This means eating the right foods and doing her best to avoid chemicals that can interfere with the baby's development. Cigarette smoke, alcohol and certain types of medicine can all damage a growing fetus.

When the baby is fully developed and ready to leave the womb, cells in the baby's brain release a chemical which travels in the baby's blood and then through the connection with the mother's blood. This chemical is a signal from the baby's body to the mother's body. Once it arrives, the muscles of the womb begin to squeeze and push the baby out into the world so it can start on the next step of its life plan.

Many mothers say that when they see and hold their baby they are filled with a special feeling of love. Perhaps this is also part of the life plan.

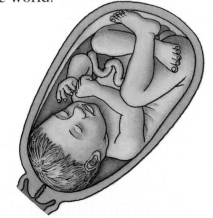

39 weeks:
This is the ideal stage for the baby to leave its mother's womb and begin life in the outside world.

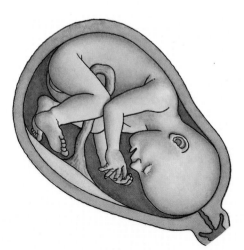

24 weeks:
Babies born at this stage have survived, but they usually need a great deal of medical help at a special premature baby intensive care unit.

Doing, learning and growing

Newborn humans are completely helpless. For the next stage in their life plan, they need to be cared for by older people and the way they are cared for has an important effect on the course of their life plan.

Most people living in Britain today were well fed when they were growing up, but in the past many parents couldn't afford to give their children enough of the right kinds of food. The difference that a good diet makes to the way people grow can be seen by looking at the skeletons and health records of our ancestors. One study showed that the people living in Glasgow one hundred years ago were, on average, a foot shorter than the people living there today.

Poorly nourished children can't grow and develop as well as children who are given enough of the right kinds of food.

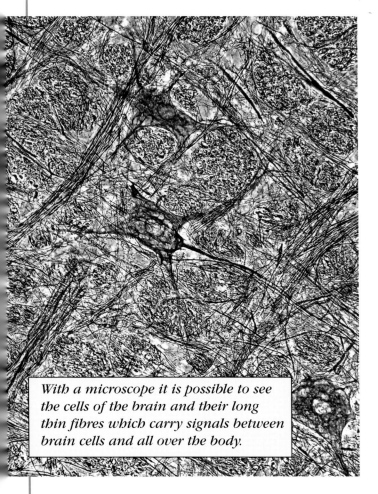

With a microscope it is possible to see the cells of the brain and their long thin fibres which carry signals between brain cells and all over the body.

Babies and children need more than food and shelter as they are growing up. They also need to be played with and talked to. When a baby is in its mother's womb, millions of connections form between its brain and the other parts of its body. Cells in the brain and spine grow long thin nerve fibres which extend through the body to touch a cell or group of cells. They create a network of nerves carrying signals between the brain and every part of the body. After the baby is born it has to learn to use that network to control its body and to receive and understand information from the outside world.

How the brain develops is still very much a mystery, but it seems to involve brain cells making connections with one another. When you were about three months old, you started to want to touch and grab at things. Your family held out rattles and toys for you to reach for. You weren't very good at first, but you learned from your mistakes. In time, the right connections formed in your brain, the muscles in your arm grew stronger and picking things up became easy.

The way that babies behave, what they learn and how they grow is a perfectly organised part of the human life plan. As a baby approaches six months of age, people warn new parents to move things to high shelves and lockable cupboards because the baby will soon be crawling around putting everything in its mouth.

When a toddler has temper tantrums, people say, 'Don't worry that's normal for two year olds.'

Babies go through the stages at slightly different ages, of course, but if they seem too far off schedule, people begin to worry that something may be wrong.

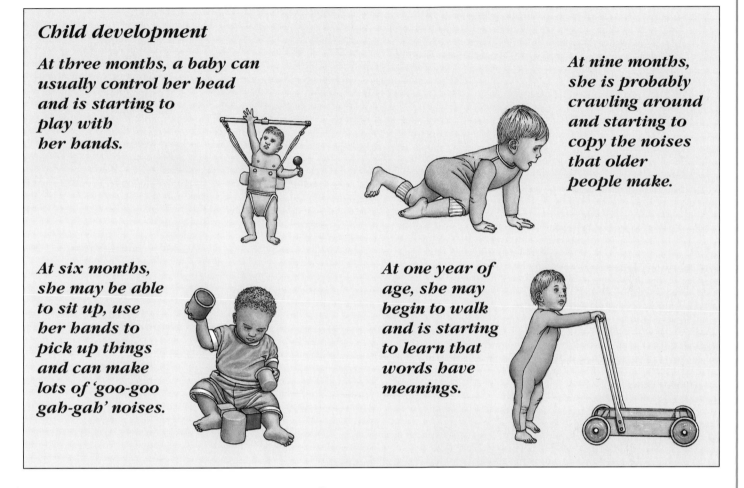

Child development

At three months, a baby can usually control her head and is starting to play with her hands.

At nine months, she is probably crawling around and starting to copy the noises that older people make.

At six months, she may be able to sit up, use her hands to pick up things and can make lots of 'goo-goo gah-gah' noises.

At one year of age, she may begin to walk and is starting to learn that words have meanings.

The cells that protect you from disease also have to learn from their experiences as you grow up. Their job is to destroy the bacteria and viruses that invade your body and clear away damaged or abnormal body cells so that healthy cells can grow in their place. If a germ attacks your body, or if you have an injection to 'immunise' you against a disease-causing germ, your immune cells learn to recognise that germ and destroy it before it can do any harm.

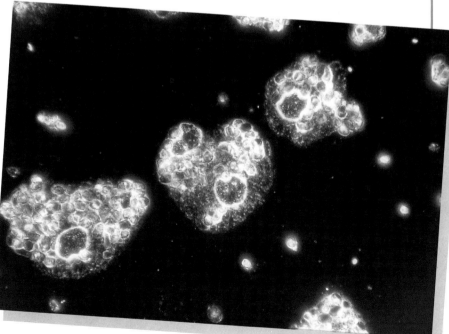

Invading germs are being eaten up by these 'macrophages'. They are part of the body's army of cells that fight infection.

Puberty

Like many mammals, human males and females look pretty much alike until a stage in the life plan called 'puberty' begins. It's a mystery how the body knows when to begin developing the ability to be a parent, but it is known that cells in the brain start the process by releasing chemical signals into the blood. These chemicals, or 'hormones', travel around the body with the blood.

For girls, puberty can begin anytime between the ages of 8 and 16. For boys, it's usually between the ages of 10 and 14. The same hormone is produced by the brains of both girls and boys, but it has a different effect because girls have ovaries and boys have testes. The cells of these organs are programmed to receive the brain's signal. As the level of the hormone increases, the cells grow and divide more quickly and in time they begin to release a chemical signal that triggers many more changes.

Puberty is also a time of changing feelings, thoughts and behaviour. It can be a very confusing time.

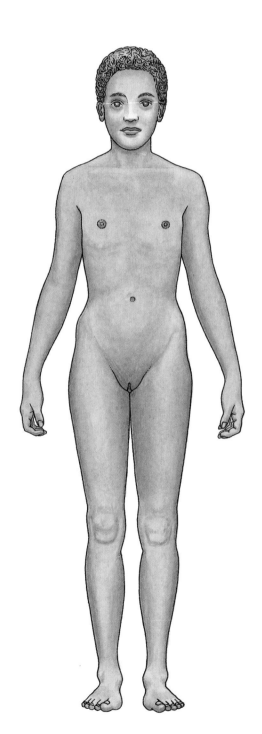

Once a girl's ovaries have grown to about ten times their previous size, they begin to make and release their own hormone called 'oestrogen'. As this travels round the girl's body in her blood, it reaches many different kinds of cell that are programmed to respond to the oestrogen signal.

Stored inside the ovaries are the girl's sex cells. Towards the end of puberty, these cells start to mature into eggs. The ovaries then begin to release one or two eggs every month or so. This monthly egg release is set to continue for the next 35 years or so, but it stops while she is pregnant or taking birth control pills.

Cells in the skin of the girl's pubic area or vulva and under her arms respond to the oestrogen signal by making a different kind of hair. Usually the first noticeable sign of puberty is the growth of these darker 'pubic' hairs. Other cells in the girl's skin start to produce more oil; spots may start to develop more often on her face.

Oestrogen triggers the cells under the skin of the girl's chest to begin to differentiate and organise themselves into tissue that will produce milk after the birth of a baby. Fat cells grow to cushion this tissue and people start to notice that the girl is developing breasts.

The growth of the girl's bones speeds up and she grows rapidly taller. Some parts of her body grow at different rates, so its proportions change. Her arms and legs and the lower part of her face become longer. These changes, along with the extra fat which grows on her hips gives her a more 'womanly' look.

Oestrogen causes the girl's womb to grow and develop, ready to provide a home for a developing baby. Every month as one of the ovaries releases an egg, the inside wall of the womb grows a soft lining that is rich in blood vessels. If the egg isn't fertilised, the lining is released and the girl has a period.

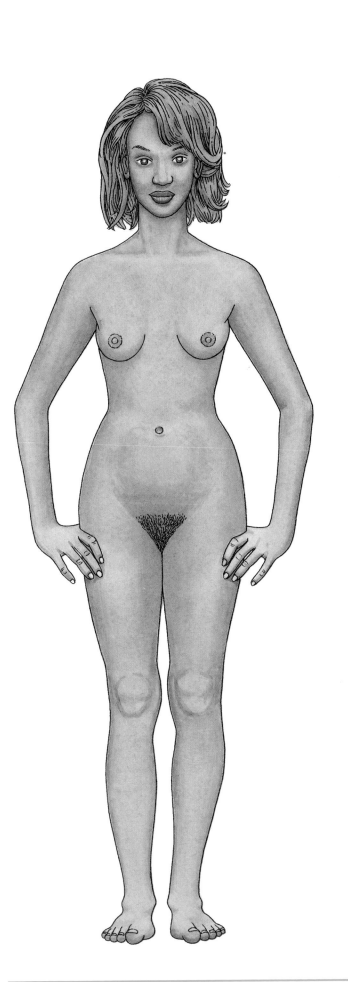

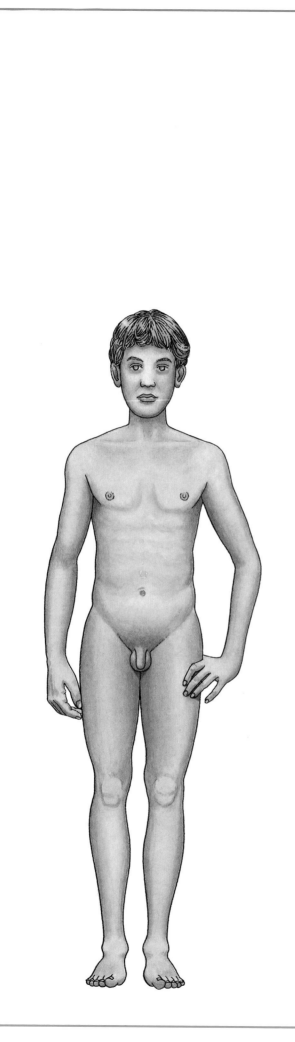

Often the first sign of puberty a boy notices is that his testes are starting to grow larger. As they do, they begin to make and release the hormone 'testosterone'. Testosterone travels around the body in the blood, reaching many different kinds of cells that are programmed to respond to its signal.

The testes also start to make sperm, the boy's sex cells, up to 200 million of them every day. They are stored in the testes and released in a gush of fluid called an 'ejaculation'.

Testosterone triggers the penis to grow longer and wider. The penis gets larger temporarily from time to time, too. This is caused by more blood flowing into the penis and is called having an erection. It happens to boys before puberty, but once puberty starts it usually occurs more frequently. Having an erection makes it possible for the penis to reach right inside a woman's vagina during sex so that sperm can be released inside her.

Cells in the skin above the penis respond to the testosterone signal by growing hair that is darker and longer. In time, skin cells under the arms, on the face and other parts of the body also grow new hair. Some boys become much hairier than others. Other cells in the skin start to make more sweat and oil; boys often start to develop spots during puberty.

Testosterone triggers a rapid growth of bones and muscles causing a dramatic growth spurt. Some boys grow as much as 13cm (5 inches) in a single year. The arms and legs grow the most and the body takes on a more manly shape as the shoulders become broad and muscular compared to the hips.

The part of a boy's throat that contains the vocal cords also responds to the testosterone signal by growing larger and the sound the cords make becomes lower in pitch. Everyone notices that the boy's voice has 'broken'; he has the deeper voice of a man.

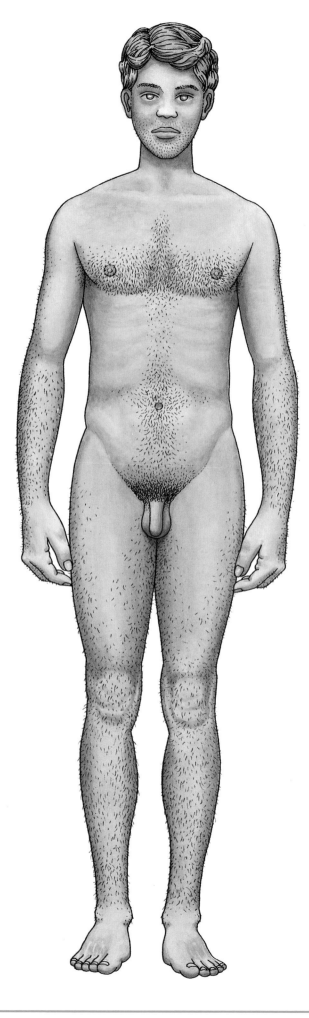

Becoming a parent

To be a parent, you need to make special sex cells. In females these are eggs and they are made in the ovaries. In males, they are sperm and are made in the testes. Unlike the cells that make up your body, sex cells don't carry the complete set of genetic instructions which are used to make your body. Body cells actually carry a double set of instrucions, one inherited from your mother, the other from your father. Sex cells contain only a single set of instructions made up of different combinations of the information from your mother and father.

On the right is an egg (coloured pink) that has just been released from the ovary. Below are sperm (coloured white) in the testes.Once released, their long tails allow them to swim toward the egg.

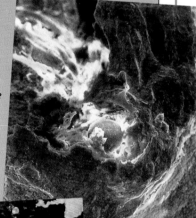

To become a parent, you also have to have sex so that egg and sperm can join inside the body of the female and the first cell of the new person can be created. One of the biggest mysteries of our life plan is how the mind develops to make us attracted to other people, to want to have sex with them, to love them and to want to take on the responsibility of raising a family.

Threads of fate

The children of Ancient Greece were told that the course of each person's life is decided by a thread. Three goddesses called the Fates made the thread, measured its length and cut it.

As scientists learned more about how living things grow and develop, they became sure that the cells must be following some sort of instructions. They discovered that these instructions, which they call 'genetic information', are stored in the structure of a chemical called 'deoxyribonucleic acid' or DNA for short. This chemical, which is in the cells of all living things, is in the form of long thin molecules and when DNA is extracted from cells, it looks like thread.

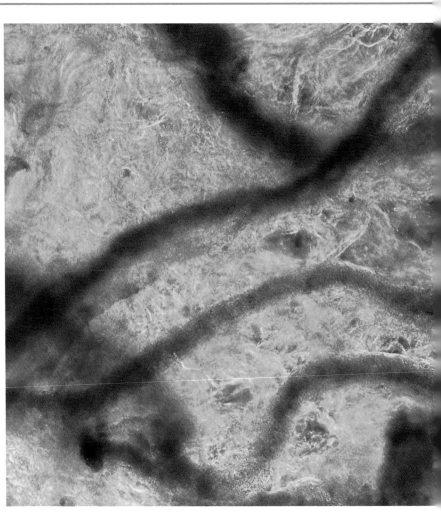

DNA carries the plans for the chemicals that make up the structure and working parts of each cell. Because all your cells grew from a single cell, they all carry the same information. The basic outline of the life plan is written in your DNA. By following the information written in your DNA, your cells organized themselves into a human being which looks more or less like other human beings. But, unless you have an identical twin, the information on your DNA is slightly different from anyone else's and it is the differences in these threads of fate that account for many of the differences between people.

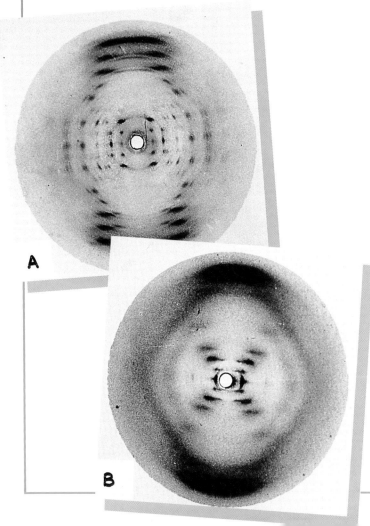

A

B

This pattern was made by X-rays shining through a crystal of DNA. A scientist called Rosalind Franklin took these pictures in the early 1950s when scientists were just beginning to suspect the importance of DNA. With the help of these pictures, she and other scientists were able to work out the molecular structure of DNA. Since then, our understanding of the instructions coded on DNA has slowly increased as scientists all over the world work together to learn how living things work.

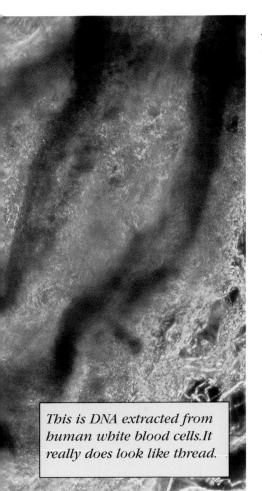

This is DNA extracted from human white blood cells. It really does look like thread.

Just as you do not look exactly the same as other people, the course of your life plan will not be the same either. Since you inherited your genetic instructions from your parents, you probably look like them and you may be similar in other ways as well.

The choices you make, the kind of family you grow up in and plain old luck will all influence how your life will turn out. But the threads of fate in your cells will have some influence as well. You won't become a tall slim catwalk model or a champion sprinter if you didn't inherit from your parents the genetic instructions for building those kinds of bodies. The information written in your DNA will also influence the kinds of illnesses you will suffer as you go through life and whether or not you are destined to live to an old age.

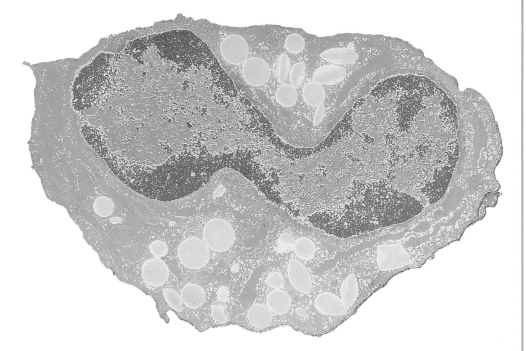

This is a human white blood cell magnified 6500 times. In the cells of more complicated living things, the DNA (coloured green) is usually kept separate from the rest of the cell in a part of the cell called 'the nucleus' (coloured red). The DNA may seem to be in a tangle but the cell is still able to find the instructions it needs.

Growing older

After puberty, the human body is mature. As long as it remains healthy, it won't change in any important way for many years. The human mind keeps developing though.

Connections between the cells in the brain keep on being built and broken down. Some of these changes may be programmed as part of the life plan but changes in the brain are also influenced by experiences. Growing older usually means seeing more of the world, meeting new people and taking on the responsibility of looking after a family. Learning and coping with new experiences causes changes in personality and attitude to life.

As the years pass, people begin to look older. Many quite small changes contribute to this older look but most noticeably, skin becomes more wrinkled and hair turns grey. Looking older can bring a person increased respect. It's a sign of the years of experience the person has had. But some older people fear that the signs of ageing show that they are worn out. Many people dye their grey hair and a few even have operations to smooth their wrinkled skin.

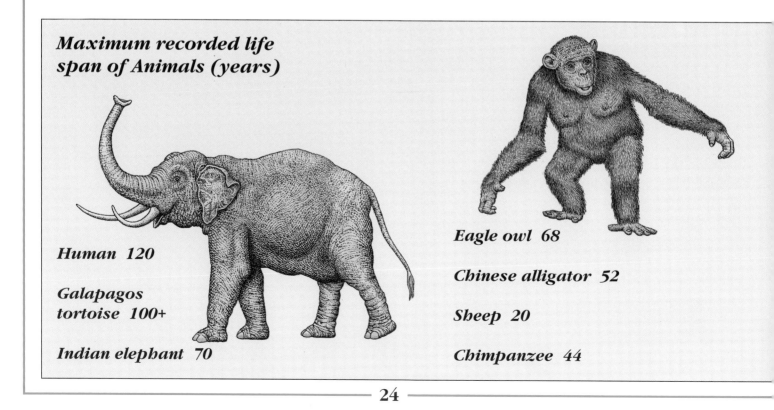

Maximum recorded life span of Animals (years)

Human 120

Galapagos tortoise 100+

Indian elephant 70

Eagle owl 68

Chinese alligator 52

Sheep 20

Chimpanzee 44

Hiding the signs of ageing can make people feel more confident, but it can't make them younger. However, most people still feel young and healthy long after they've stopped looking young. Being older doesn't mean a person is no longer useful and it doesn't mean they can't have fun. The problem is, although no one knows exactly what their future holds, everyone knows that as the body ages it will stop working so well and, in time, it will stop working altogether.

Humans appear to be the only animals that know the fate that lies in store for them as they grow older, but we are not the only animal to have a limited life span. Some insects live only a few days. Humans are the longest lived of the mammals.

Keeping fit and eating the right kinds of foods gives people a better chance of staying healthy, but it is no guarantee. Illness still strikes people who take care of their bodies.

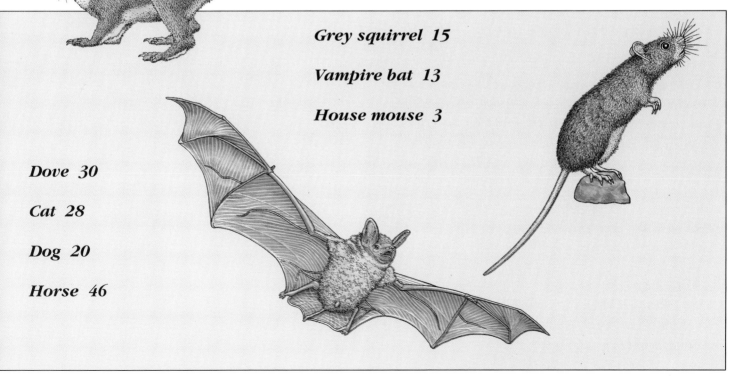

Grey squirrel 15

Vampire bat 13

House mouse 3

Dove 30

Cat 28

Dog 20

Horse 46

Many scientists think that old bodies don't work as well as younger ones for the same reason that cars and refrigerators don't work as well when they're old as when they're new. Just being alive causes a lot of wear and tear. Cells are constantly being damaged by ultraviolet rays from the sun and other radiation from Earth and from space. Our food and water and the air we breathe contain many chemicals and some of them can harm cells. Simply using our bones and muscles causes stress and strain and this is bound to damage them.

Cells are able to repair this damage but it builds up over time making it harder to keep the body working well. It's more efficient to produce brand new bodies and this is what animals do. Animals have survived for millions of years not by having long-lasting bodies but by making babies. An animal's cells need to be good at repairing themselves, but only good enough to keep the body going until it has made its replacements. Humans need cells that are particularly good at repairing themselves because it takes many years to raise human children.

The pain, heat and redness of sunburn soon go away, but the ultraviolet radiation from the Sun also causes invisible damage to the skin which is more difficult to repair.

Some ways the body changes as it gets older:

From about the age of 20 everyone loses about 10,000 brain cells every day. This means over 200 million are lost by the age of 80 but this still leaves the brain with a lot of cells (about 10,000 million cells).

Old bodies are more likely to suffer from diseases such as arthritis and cancer.

The mass of muscles and bones starts to decrease and this also make hard exercise more difficult.

Scientists have found some intriguing evidence that the story of ageing is more complicated than this. Our cells may be programmed to let our bodies deteriorate when we're old just as they're programmed to go through the earlier stages in our life plan. Our cells are programmed to shut themselves down and die under certain conditions. Cell death helps to shape the developing embryo (look back to page 12) and throughout our lives, older cells die as their replacements are ready.

More surprising is that even cells which are grown in a laboratory seem programmed to die. Researchers can take small samples of cells from a person's body and keep them alive in bottles containing a solution of nutrients. Many types of body cell stay healthy and keep growing and dividing in these conditions, but only for a while. After dividing a certain number of times, the cells always stop growing and die. Cells from an animal with a short life span, a mouse for instance, don't live as long as human cells. And, even more fascinating, cells taken from a child stay alive longer and divide more times than cells from an old person. The cells may no longer be part of the person but they still seem to be timing how much life the person's cells have left.

Some scientists believe they've found clues showing how each cell's 'clock' works. Inside the nucleus of the cell, at each tip of each long DNA thread called a chromosome is a special section that seems to protect it. The scientists have found that these endpieces become a tiny bit shorter each time the cell divides. Perhaps, when they get too short the cell can no longer divide and shuts down, or dies.

Living human cells can be frozen temporarily, but it may never be possible to freeze a living human body safely.

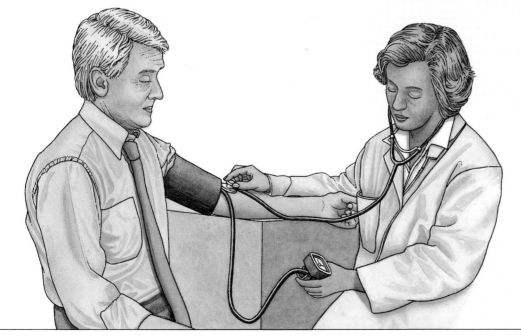

The arteries that carry blood to the different parts of the body become narrower and less flexible in most old people. This makes it harder for them to do strenuous work and more likely to have a heart attack or stroke.

Can we cheat fate?

The Ancient Greeks may have believed that people should accept what fate has in store for them, but people today often don't. Why should they? Science and technology have given us the power to change so many things that we find unacceptable. It used to be quite common for babies and children to die. Living in dirty overcrowded homes and not having enough to eat makes children easy victims of infectious diseases.

When we see people who are less fortunate than ourselves, such as these children in a Rio de Janeiro shanty town, most of us feel the need to help.

It seems wrong not to try to help others, especially when providing something simple, like a water pump, can bring such a big improvement to some people's lives.

Today, in most industrialised countries, it is very unusual for a child to die of an infection and most people believe we should try to help children all over the world to grow up healthy. The rich people of the world may not be very good at sharing their wealth, but few people would say that the poor should just accept their fate. But what happens when that fate is written in their DNA? Doctors have no doubt that the length of a person's life is linked to the genetic information that children inherit from their parents.

Most healthy old people had parents and grandparents who also lived a long healthy life. Many ill people have ancestors who suffered from the same diseases.

For some diseases, the link with the genetic instructions is clear. Scientists have found the small mistakes in genetic instructions that cause cystic fibrosis, thalassaemia and some other inherited diseases. In many more common medical problems (asthma, diabetes, arthritis, heart disease and cancer, for example) the link is not so clear but these diseases are also known to run in families.

There are already treatments for these conditions but many scientists are hopeful that really effective ways of preventing and curing them could be developed soon. Biologists are now able to read the genetic instructions written on the cell's DNA and they are finding out more about how these instructions are linked to poor health and growing older. They are beginning to try out new ways of replacing pieces of DNA which carry mistakes. As their understanding increases, they may find ways of using this 'genetic engineering' to cure or prevent many illnesses.

It may also be possible to find ways of using this 'genetic engineering' to allow people to change things about themselves that they just don't like. Bald people may be able to grow hair. Short people may be able to grow tall. Parents may be able to have children with a better chance of being great athletes or super intelligent. And as we learn more about what happens to the body as we grow older, we may find ways of slowing down ageing or at least preventing many of the diseases that people can suffer from as they grow older.

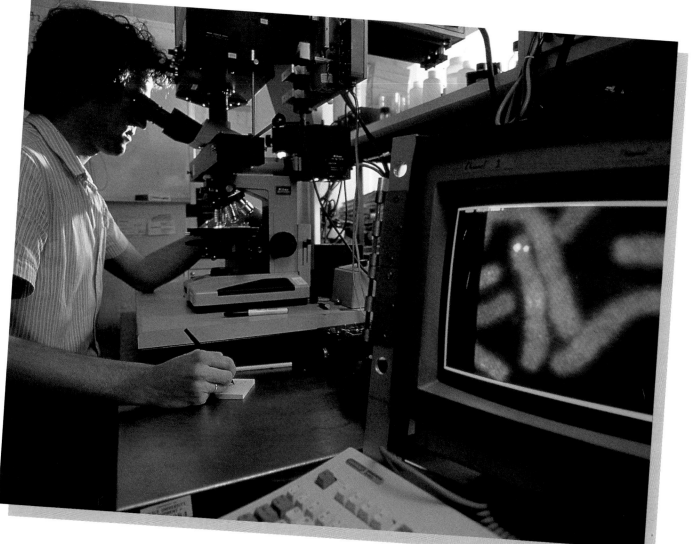

When doctors see people who are unfortunate enough to have
a mistake in their genetic information which makes them unhealthy, they would like to help.
Scientists are working to locate these mistakes and are trying to find ways of repairing them.

It's already possible to make changes to the human life plan by altering the levels of certain hormones. A small number of children don't make enough of the hormone that stimuates growth. In the past there was no scientific help available to people with this problem. Today such children can have injections of growth hormone and reach normal height. A few doctors have also given hormone injections to stimulate the growth of children who don't have a medical problem but are simply destined to be short because their parents are short.

This 11 year-old boy was destined to be what people used to call a 'midget' because his body doesn't produce enough growth hormone. But doctors are now able to give him injections of extra growth hormone and this will make it possible for him to grow to a normal height.

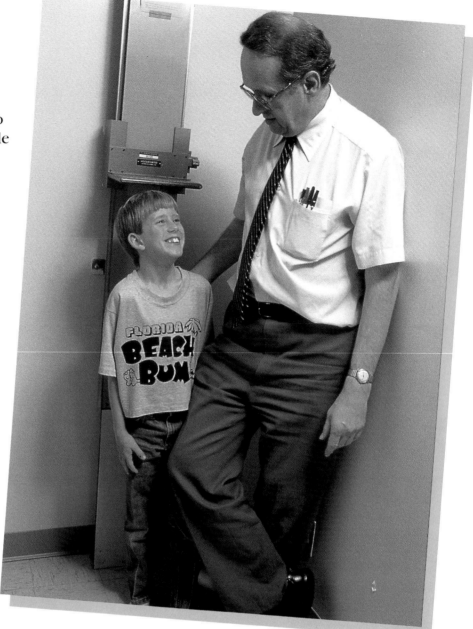

It's now quite common for women to use hormone treatment to take greater control of their lives. According to the human life plan, a young woman who is not pregnant is very likely to get pregnant if she has sex regularly. Every month or so she releases an egg. But today, if a woman doesn't want to get pregnant, she can take birth control pills. The hormones these pills contain stop her ovaries releasing eggs.

When her store of eggs is used up, a woman goes through what is called 'the menopause'. Her periods stop and her ovaries begin releasing less and less of the hormone oestrogen. Many women begin taking hormone replacement therapy or HRT when the menopause starts.

HRT replaces the oestrogen that her ovaries are no longer releasing. The oestrogen can be taken in tablets or the woman can wear a sticky skin patch that gradually releases the hormone through her skin.

Many women say that they begin to feel more tired and frail after their periods stop. Medical research has also shown that women are more likely to have a heart attack or stroke, break a bone or develop cancer after the menopause. Having HRT seems to make quite a few women feel much better and some doctors are hopeful that HRT may help prevent or at least delay the medical problems that women suffer as they get older.

On the other hand, there are also many women who feel perfectly well after menopause. Some women try HRT and stop quickly saying it makes them feel worse. Some don't have HRT because they believe it isn't right to interfere with something that is just a normal part of growing older.

A woman must feel well to enjoy the tiring job of helping to look after her grandchildren.

A purpose to the plan?

For many centuries people made sense of suffering by believing it to be part of a 'larger life plan'. Have scientific discoveries ruled out that idea? Almost all scientists believe that the human life plan was worked out over billions of years as our ancestors evolved from simpler forms of life. Some people think that evolution is the 'larger life plan' into which our individual life plans fit, but among scientists there is the same mixture of ideas and beliefs as there is among non-scientists. Some believe there may be a greater purpose into which life, death and evolution fit and no scientific discovery has ruled this out.

Humans have always felt a need to understand the joy and suffering that life brings.

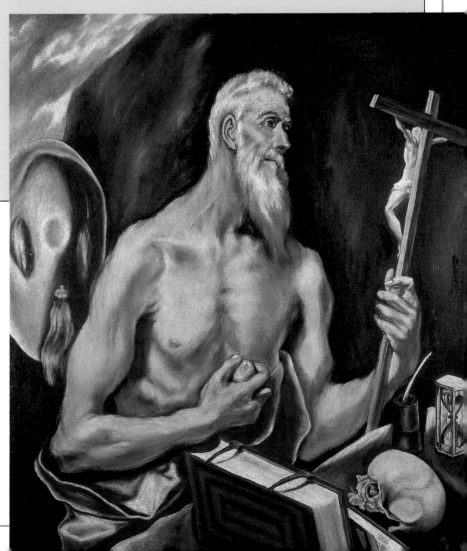

It may be possible to make changes to the life plan written in our DNA but is it right to do so? The human life plan is able to turn single cells into wise old men and women. We may understand a little about how the plan works, but it is still amazing and mysterious. Is it wise to tamper with it? On the other hand, if people are in misery because they are sick, old or even just because they are short, shouldn't doctors and scientists try to help them?

Acknowledgements

The author and publisher would like to thank Sarah Codrington, Nuffield Science Curriculum Projects Centre; Sidney Shall, Laboratory of Cell and Molecular Biology; Prof Raymond Tallis, Dept of Geriatric Medicine Hope Hospital; Prof Tom Kirkwood, University of Manchester; Colin Tudge, London School of Economics; Andrew Copp, Institute of Child Health; Prof Marshall Marinker, MSD Ltd.

Photographic credits
Front cover clockwise from bottom right: Alex Bartel/Science Photo Library, Chris Fairclough, Peter Menzel/Science Photo Library, Chris Fairclough; Back cover (top) Judy Harrison/ Format, (bottom) Dr Maurice Cross

p2 Courtesy of Nottingham Museums, Castle Museum and Art Gallery; p3 (top) Chris Fairclough, (bottom) Simon Fraser/Science Photo Library; p4 (top) CM Dixon, (bottom) Mary Evans Picture Library; p5 Bhaktivedanta Book Trust; p6 (top) Science Photo Library, (bottom) Manfred Kage/ Science Photo Library; p7 (top) Dr Gopal Murti/ Science Photo Library; p8 Dr George Gornacz/ Science Photo Library; p9 (top) Chris Fairclough, (bottom) Weiss/Jerrican/Science Photo Library; p10 National Shire Horse Centre; p11 Dr Lloyd Beidler/Science Photo Library; p12 Petit Format/Nestle/Science Photo Library; p13 Philippe Plailly/Science Photo Library; p14 (top) David Leah (Science Photo Library), (bottom) Harris Birthright Research Centre; p15 Bubbles/Ian West; p16 (top) Mary Evans Picture Library, (bottom) Manfred Kage/Science Photo Library; p17 Cecil H. Fox/Science Photo Library; p18 Graham Horner/Chapel Studios; p21 (top) Professors P Motta and J van Blerkom/Science Photo Library, (bottom) Professor P Motta/ Science Photo Library; p22 (top) Philippe Plailly/ Science Photo Library, (bottom) Rosalind Franklin, with the permission of King's College, London; p23 (top) Bubbles/F Rombout, (bottom) Dr Gopal Murti/Science Photo Library; p24 Zul Mukhida/Chapel Studios; p25 Jerry Wachter/Science Photo Library; p26 Sinclair Stammers/Science Photo Library; p27 Francoise Sauze/ Science Photo Library; p28 (top) Mark Edwards/ Still Pictures, (bottom) Jorgen Schytte/Still Pictures; p29 Peter Menzel/Science Photo Library; p30 Will and Deni McIntyre/Science Photo Library; p31 (top) Bubbles/ F Rombout, (bottom) Prado, Madrid/Bridgeman Art Library, London

First published 1996

A & C Black (Publishers) Limited
35 Bedford Row
London WC1R 4JH

ISBN 0-7136-4027-8

© A & C Black (Publishers) Limited

A CIP catalogue record for this book is available from the British Library.

Illustrations by Jason Lewis

Index